"This ground breaking anthology of international voices traverse the breadth and depth of queer experience."

Mary Jean Chan, author of *Flèche*

"So many poets I admire in one place! *The Sun Isn't Out Long Enough*, despite being an English language anthology, is internationally-minded and full of furious lyricism, experiments in forms, translations and conversations. Acquaint yourself with excellence."

Raymond Antrobus, author of *All the Names Given*

"*The Sun Isn't Out Long Enough* is an anthology that queers the notion of queer. For these writers, queerness is both a mirror and window to other worlds only made possible because of their resistance to the violently conventional, the stubbornly closed-off. Here, borders dissolve in the capaciousness of queerness, making these poems and prose pieces a diaspora that stings, reveals, and holds close."

Phillip B. Williams, author of *Mutiny*

"These are the writers who invent themselves in language, in bodily experience, in breath moving into expression. Here are the words that could help you live."

Kazim Ali, author of *The Voice of Sheila Chandra*

First published by Anamot Press 2021
www.anamotpress.com

ISBN 978-1-5272-9421-9

Cover illustration by Yannick Scott
Edited by Tatevik Sargsyan
Typeset in Palatino and Albertus

Printed and bound by Henry Ling Limited in Dorchester, Dorset, UK

Supported using public funding by the National Lottery through Arts Council England.

Supported using public funding by

LOTTERY FUNDED

ARTS COUNCIL ENGLAND

THE SUN ISN'T OUT LONG ENOUGH

Edited by Tatevik Sargsyan

Anamot Press
London

CONTENTS

'Perhaps home is not a place but simply an irrevocable condition'

James Baldwin

Introduction

TATEVIK SARGSYAN

Anamot (Անամօթ) means shameless in Armenian. Shame is universal, we can all relate to it. Shame can gather in your throat, under the tongue, in the caves of your armpits, and it emerges at borderlands and in transit. So many of our desires and experiences are labelled, blamed and shamed. Yet, shame doesn't like to be shared. I established Anamot Press in order to publish queer experiences and other stories told with no shame, foregrounding but not limited to those of us who migrate and have diasporic roots and tendrils.

The Sun Isn't Out Long Enough is the first anthology and explores a range of themes spanning queerness and language, belonging and loss, the embodiment of ancestral grief, liminal love and diasporic desires. The poems and prose in this book are as diverse as the international writers themselves. The title of the anthology is from the opening poem by Andriniki Mattis. I feel it's an evocation of the liminal spaces that queerness moves through. Queer experiences connected through firsts and lasts; how the same sun sets differently and is experienced differently depending on our perspective of the horizon. Sunsets are both joyful and regretful. They are both arriving and letting go; seemingly having long enough time until you don't. Shame gathers in the shadows. It is hidden in the crevices of the body and contained in the contours of the sun's shadows.

Poetry is important to me because it's how I learn language. Reading poetry is like a mark in time; minutes and hours become totally recomposed. I set up Anamot Press a week before the first national lockdown was announced in the UK. As the global pandemic ensued so did a multitude of experiences: it was a compounding time of re-emerging ancestral grief and oppression of Armenian people in Artsakh (and elsewhere), continuous familial and diasporic guilt, queer desire and love, and a muting of language to embody a chaotic space.

In the same week, on World Poetry Day, poet Mary Jean Chan reflected that: "Now more than ever, I turn to poetry for its propensity towards truth, its tensile strength, and its insistence that language can, and must be, the bridge that connects us all during these difficult times." I found solace in poetry during the pandemic—a time where life was held in abeyance—as the practice of reading and reflecting on poetry is both expansive and implosive, casting out threads which weave into new perspectives.

I offer this anthology as both a talisman and a gift: it shares queer experiences across borders and other stories, with no shame.

Foreword

MARY JEAN CHAN

Ten years ago, I came out as queer. In the months that followed, I experienced the five stages of grief: denial, anger, bargaining, depression and acceptance. Looking back, I wish I could have turned to a book like *The Sun Isn't Out Long Enough* for inspiration, strength and solace, because it achieves what the best kind of writing is capable of, by reminding the reader that they are not alone. The poetry and prose in this groundbreaking anthology of international voices traverse the breadth and depth of queer experience, echoing Samir Dayal's astute observation that queerness goes beyond sexual orientation to a "queering of the pitch, a displacement of colonial, heteronormative, or otherwise hegemonic stratifications." Similarly, Sara Ahmed contends that "race [is] a rather queer matter". This anthology represents a growing awareness among writers, editors and publishers that power asymmetries persist within queer spaces, and that a multitude of marginalised voices remain unheard within queer Anglophone writing, especially that which is published in the Global North. As such, this anthology attempts to begin to redress this issue by featuring a range of writers whose work centres on – or is shaped by – migration, liminal identities and diasporic desires.

In particular, the poets in this anthology embody the wondrous complexity of queer lives across borders. By refusing to be tokenised or stereotyped, they offer up powerful glimpses of queer survival, resistance and rage, as well as desire, love and joy during a time of multiple crises worldwide, ranging from the ecological to the social and political. In the poem from which this anthology derives its title, Andriniki Mattis writes: "it's the year 2020 / & pandemically speaking / you have never felt so close to death / it disturbs you enough to wonder / if it will be you or someone you love". In a time of grief, suffering and loss, what struck me most as I read and re-read these poems is the sheer vitality that runs through each and every verse: "oh, the green / snake love makes of you" (Jody Chan); "I never believed in God, but when I fell / face first into a pit of snow, all I felt was warmth" (Noor Hindi); "The way we crave / Contour and reaction / Language and the body" (Joshua Escobar); "Your name in full is a speech act in movement" (Ximena Keogh Serrano); "Every day is an invitation into intimacy, I decide, leaving my house" (Taylor Johnson). These poets and others in this book bring to mind June Jordan's enduring words: "I am not sure any longer that there is a difference between writing and living." For queer writers, this is doubly true, as we cannot help but bring all of who we are to the page. In an interview, Natalie Diaz observes: "Language is urgent. Living is urgent. I must do them." The writers in this anthology sculpt language into being, such that the reader is invited to experience their work with the presence of our full humanity.

ANDRINIKI MATTIS

the sun isn't out long enough

the pitch black from outside plays against the clouds in your chest
the wreckage of it all leaves you
& you wake in the morning
dressing for the arrival of a new you
who talks like you & looks like you but happier & charming

you say to yourself how did we get here
you count all the lines in your palms & every tattoo etched into you

you find a piece of metal welded together that fits the nape of your neck
yet you are not a cyborg
it's the year 2020
& pandemically speaking
you have never felt so close to death
it disturbs you enough to wonder
if it will be you or someone you love
or someone you met at a bookstore or your first friend from college or your
fifth grade teacher
or your neighbor across the street with the great dane or the person you
were supposed to meet
three years ago at a festival or the passenger next to you on the plane who
reminds you of your
mother
or your mother

& then you wake up & do your job & do your life & then it's 7 months then
ten then vaccine
& then the why so many deaths & then it's fall then the winter & the story
writes itself now
& the administration will be blamed in the book you haven't read yet
that will be out in five years
that you'll hear of in a group chat about divesting from capitalism
& a knot grows in your throat as you realize there is no grid to fall off of
& no country to have you but your own

ANDRINIKI MATTIS

masc

I wanted so much to be strong
to hold down the tide below my knees
I blew my heart straight out of my body
& couldn't put it back
I planted my head into my chest
because it was all the same to me
I dreamed so much of a day
when this body would bring me peace
no more headaches
no more nostalgia of a time
that was not my own
I never wanted it to be so heavy
the ribbons the frills the girlish charm the swooning skirts
I fed it all to the fire
all that would not own me any longer
I sip whiskey without a grimace
let chin hairs grow
& let my voice deepen
paint my nails in rebellion of it all
because it could never be so cut or dry
this womanhood this manhood this binary bequeathed to me
oh my queer queer heart
at it again trying to outdo the boys on the jungle gym
only to hear the womanhood put upon me
steadying my shoulders
closing my legs
folding them into envelopes of do's and do not's
I never stood a chance
so I depart from both instead with a bold whimper
sit through this theyhood a meditation on not giving a fuck

GOLNOOSH NOUR

Ode to Self

We survived and survival breeds desire for more self. – Audre Lorde

I am that
the fatigued knight wading through the morning light
like Moses gaping the Nile

I am that
the black rose in winter, dead
butterflies dripping from my bruised petals.

I am it
The 'it factor', the cool factor minus, the cold factor plus, the hot
mess, the browned flesh, the queer crushed
by Authority, forever refusing to agree with anything
other than my own elegant violence, my
autumnal tendencies that I catch in the river of my mirror – the only truth teller

for I am that,
the breathing painting in the attic
the 'darling' collector
the cold sore in summer
the sore throat in spring
the allergy screeching at the skin.

I am it
the blue silk with a scarlet kernel,
wrapped in my gold cape, embroidered by thorns, I pounce
over the fence into the abyss to caress
my horns, and to plant myself in fertile soil, roots hard in the ground;
shaking off tornados from my trembling naked branches, I grow tall,
old, short, skyward, enamoured,
pure.

GOLNOOSH NOUR

Lost Cult

Lingering like smoke, I end
up in a broken park. Colourful flowers
scattered, like the toys of a mad toddler,
a bright curse that stalks my skin.

A poet murmurs, 'It is desire that
makes you follow someone in
the dark, to paths untrodden.'
And I have an epiphany;

A long time ago, she followed me
down a leafy corridor; two women
exhuming Eros but heading nowhere;
how could the innocent me accept

that the person I desired the most,
desired me also? O she whom I
worshipped. She who would've killed
me, drinking my cunt.

GOLNOOSH NOUR

Cliff Trip

Our trip ends when our screams turn
to silence. The silence a precipice from which I fall
as she grabs my hand halfway and I
mumble, 'Our time together is jewel.'

She snickers. She wants to share it with all the rats
she collects in her wooden aquarium
and when I tell her I am allergic to rats and
addicted to cats, she shuts me up by calling me a snob.

Our tears fall indistinguishable in the rain over the
precipice. I attempt to breathe while falling
but her ruthless rats attack sucking my little blood
I am not falling; I fell off this cliff a long time ago.

She stares at me, her eyes dark like fire
and she states my selfishness is killing
our love. I stay silent, knowing my selfishness
is the only thing that has kept me alive.

JODY CHAN

semantic satiation

a hunger claims your morning run, a sudden need
to know the exact angle of your ankles' trajectory,
if each footfall chips a little from the knee, if
she still crosswords at this precise hour, if in a year any of this
would mean anything at all. mouth-up on the couch, your almost-
love spews inappropriately at another who can't reciprocate. why didn't she
choose me, you ask. you were never skilled at waiting, always
slithering mouth-first into the wading pool of your madness. girl
        unrequited. neckless
girl, girl until wet, then the other end
            of an attempted overdose. wet cheeks, wet grass,
wet pillow underneath your open jaw. oh, the green
snake love makes of you. love, or what you have learned to call this
salted, open-gullied song, wet as a mouth. at the supermarket, almost-dead
fish gape from plastic nets, blood trickling through ice. what
magic it is to feed another with your body. what madness your body,
a highway mounted west
        in both directions.
shapeshifter, as in, the way you say mouth
            too many times and it becomes a mirror.

JODY CHAN

palinode

for three hours, you tried to sleep
the night outside hung wetly like a tongue
two moths darted into the bathroom
~~she said call me if you start to struggle~~
your lover slept on the other side of a window
when you woke up you were still   they prodded
your awakeness like a door   a heavy wind entered through
their mouth   a moth
curtained your eyes, blood-blue
you had never been more
loved   you took the pills, then you woke up
your friends observed you from behind a windshield
from your phone, the far room, just down the block
~~you dropped~~ three blue pills
fell between the cedar decking boards
of the ten you extracted from the plastic bottle
you begged her not to call
the cops   you found two moths orbiting
light, one singed wetly on the bulb
your friends would not let you sleep alone
the moth-swollen night, the sound of wind
rustling a single leaf
when you woke up, you were still alive
you   drank the glass with your bare hands
heavy with blue, the dead
grass howls   the odour of toothpaste, mixed with cinnamon
you begged them not to call
the doctor   you had never loved
your lover more   a whisper of moths, a swollen
window   you recall it took nearly an hour
to tell her   how your voice cracked
the wind in two, how the ceiling above you shut its eyes
in shame, how you slept the whole way home

NOOR HINDI

Poem in Which My Feelings Fuck Each Other Into More Feelings

Close your office door // don't leave me //
a voicemail // I can't unstuck myself // from wild wild wild //
dear sadness // didn't you hear // I killed the moon dear poets // look
at my beautiful // show of language // I twist my words // my languish //
oops oops oops my language // my knuckles
// my silly trauma // my yellow kite // oh god // there it is again
// dear god // please leave
// the clouds alone // no need to cry
today // I'm better // I'm song & soft & snug // like mourn // stomp stomp
there are coffins & coffins & coffins & coffins & coffins & coffins & coffins
& coffins & coffins & coffins & coffins & coffins & coffins & coffins & coffins &
coffins & coffins & coffins & coffins & coffins & coffins & coffins & coffins

oh shit — I think I love you.

NOOR HINDI

THE VOID WANTS TO KNOW HOW MY DAY IS GOING SO I TALK ABOUT THE WEATHER

Blood is warm; I miss mine. Miss my family playing Rummy until 2am. I was five and it was my birthday. Ate so many Laffy Taffy's I threw up in the kitchen. I smoke so much hookah I pass out in the kitchen. Knife in hand. Cutting a pomegranate as large as my yearning. This year is so sharp I cut corners — wound myself with worry and more worry. You were more carefree, says my cousin. Remember walking through swarms of insects. Face first. Like we owned the whole world. Like summer never ended until Zina died of a virus. Like I didn't get this text just yesterday: I think I have coronavirus. The days are too long, I argue. Translation: I'm afraid to be alive. Translation: I'm afraid to die. When Lana sings Summertime Sadness, I cry, drunk and on the verge of nothing. Keep asking questions. For what, I say? I'm sad. How else to tell you / / I hide my pride / / keychain, I hide my pride / / mask before my family asks questions. But let's talk about prayer. I never believed in God, but when I fell face first into a pit of snow, all I felt was warmth. There were lightning bugs all summer. Our trapping them an act of cruelty. My skin alive like thunder. It's hard to stay sweet. Even harder to love that which does not love you back. I don't mean to grieve so openly. On the way to Edgewater, I weep behind my sunglasses. Stare at a sun so yellow and bright I almost hate it. I want us all to make it. I want laughter as loud as rainwater. I want hugs so warm my body becomes the home I never knew.

XANDRIA PHILLIPS

WANT COULD KILL ME

I know this

from looking
                into store fronts

                taste buds voguing
alight from the way

treasure glows
                when I imagine

                pressing its opulence
into your hand

I want to buy you
                a cobalt velvet couch

                all your haters' teeth
strung up like pearls

a cannabis vineyard
                and plane tickets

                to every island
on earth

but my pockets
                are filled with

                lint and love alone

touch these inanimate gods

to my eyelids
                    when you kiss me

                    linen leather
gator skin silk

satin lace onyx
                    marble gold ferns

                    leopard crystal
sandalwood mink

pearl stiletto
                    matte nails and plush

                    lips glossed
in my 90s baby saliva

pour the glitter
                    over my bare skin

                    I want a lavish life
us in the crook

of a hammock
                    incensed by romance

                    the bowerbird will
forgo rest and meals

XANDRIA PHILLIPS

so he may primp
        and anticipate amenity

        for his singing lover
call me a gaunt bird

a keeper of altars
        shrines to the tactile

        how they shine for you
fold your wings

around my shoulders
        promise me that

        should I drown
in want-made waste

the dress I sink in
        will be exquisite

For Dominique

XANDRIA PHILLIPS

POEM WHERE I REFUSE TO TALK ABOUT ███████████

I'm eight wearing a frumpy
bunched-up dress with stockings
I put runs in that same morning
while rushing to pull them up
after peeing and flattening
my midweek temple frizz
the cool girls in their jeans
and angel | devil Ts are having
a laugh at my existence
they are white and built like
miniature bird-chested women
on asphalt my low heels
clacking like principal feet
I want the sweat of boyhood
its ease and virtue on my neck
I want my nature known
because I am the softest
I can ever be in this moment
when I don't rough my mutt
hands on their throats
for making terrible light of
the second-hand the sub
-human my survival
instead I talk to grass
but a sapling myself
I am made everyday like a bed
like a person makes another
and nothing ever asks to be made

XANDRIA PHILLIPS

YOU AND I

[NO COLONIAL]

you and I have never left ~~Nigeria Biafra~~
Yorubaland. I raise a house of children in between
kissing the maid on her lips. you,
kissing me, too. I write poems in lotion
pools in the small of your back after
our children fall asleep under the mosquito
nets. a tree drops soft fragrant fruit onto
our roof. we hear ripe thuds
in the night's quiet. I am still afraid of
snakes. bodies without limbs unsettle
me until my final days. we witness
as revolution crumbles America,
it wilts in our own city, the world
expands, and collapses
beneath our Black hands, my life
behind a memory of a colonial reality
you don't remember. each morning you wake,
your lips, your chest, your hands come down
on top of me and I flinch, remembering,
before I indulge your gentleness.

[POST COLONIAL]

the cramped apartment space we share in
these rooms, three stories up. I threaten,
secretly take a capsule every day to keep
my children waiting in either side room.
forcing penetration tires you. it only seems
droning to me, and my eyelashes cast
your lips in shadow. you admit being
only one inch above me in height,
your physical failure. it's how you comfort
my supposed barrenness. you eat
all your body will allow, and I persist.
I throw out all the gifts my body
could birth you. the day my attraction
wanes. I begin to love you, and my world
shrinks. it's the size of a human
taller than myself and all the people who
walk from my womb. I am all but
a plunging flourish of starlings
saturating the sky above in disquiet
through a partition made of circumstance.

DIANA KHOI NGUYEN

I Keep Getting Things Wrong
After Mark Levine

1

My father, just
out of his teens, stands on the rooftop
of the embassy in Saigon, his birthplace.
He gives his hand to his mother,
and all around them, a thousand hands reach up

not to wave. None of his siblings died.
Their bodies like a fine chain balled tight
in a fist. They made it out alive.
Why is he looking at me like this?

2

This is the idea of a house my father built
in Southern California. These two circle windows
and bamboo on all sides. He brought a jungle here,
complete with French doors.
These are the tiles from his mother's house, cool
against my cheek. I talk to him in one tongue,
he answers from the morgue.

3

Let's get on with it.
When I return to that house, I eat the food
left out for my dead brother. I don't waste much.
I slide open and close his closet, untangle
the window blinds. The bees are quiet in the
walls, now, their colonies dying off.
His shoes on my father's feet are the only moving thing
in sight.

DIANA KHOI NGUYEN

4

On their flight to America,
the choice for lunch was rice or pasta, but when
the meal cart reached them, there was only pasta.
My father smiled at the flight attendant and asked,
Why didn't you reap enough rice?

5

The certificates we use to be certain of each other:
ID cards, contracts, permits, deeds,
fishing licenses, driving licenses, car titles, carry permits,
registrations, income statements, IOUs, testimonials,
certificates of birth, custody, and death, letters of consent.
Do I have permission to approach
a drowning man from behind?

6

I dreamed last night, my mother says,
that you were in danger and your brother was young still,
though you were the same
as you are now.
He was looking for me and I was looking for you.

7

I sit at my desk, typing and deleting
words.
Twice I dreamed I fucked my brother.
I keep trying to wake up. I keep getting things wrong.
I'm ready to feel better.

DIANA KHOI NGUYEN

Gyotaku

uncontained even
water abandons i
tself; there is mys
tery inside migra
tion, the elver's
wimming up a
head, out of th
e photograph;
eels who ride a
top each othe
r do not have
to see each o
ther face to
face; of the
road, it doe
s not mov
e, it is eve
rywhere
it has a
a story,
I am i
n it, y
ou a
re i
n i
t

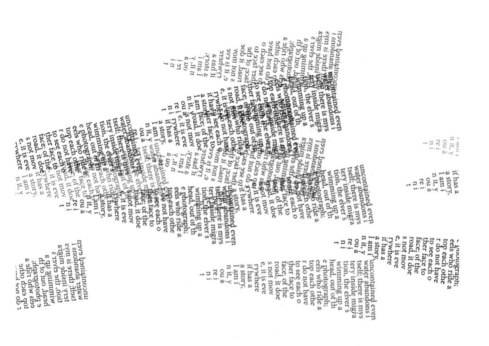

PETER SCALPELLO

The Hotline

Since I have more time on my hands
Now that my lover must work
And I gave up
I watch the hours fill
All transparency between us
Like joint aphonia
And give myself
To the job of remembering
In order
To erase

It goes like this
Each night I call the hotline
To the deceased and although
They say you know something's wrong
When the dead pick up every time
You do
And briefly
It feels like being held
Under the weight
Of compulsion

I want to talk
I want to pretend that
Acute tolerance to living
With the undesired and irreversible
Can be deciduous

When I reach you
You say something kind
Followed by something viscerally painful
Then something
Utterly mundane

PETER SCALPELLO

I just wanted you to know
As knowing is a kind of cruelty
About the boundaries I lack
And the surplus of handshakes
That wring out of me
About the nights put into
Psych bed 28
And that I lied
I don't have a lover
Irid nor decent

I just wondered if you'd heard
As herding is communion
That I am affected by the world
And the feeling isn't mutual
That I live

With desire to do bad
For the repentance that chases action
And I realise now
That you did too
Maybe it's a draw

I'm not dead
You answer and hang
Up from
Wherever you are
Hiding

I wake to the moon behind slate cloud
Still the water bends

JEE LEONG KOH

The Peace Lily
for Justin Chin
(b.1969, Kuantan, Malaysia–d.2015, San Francisco, USA)

I will sit here and think of Justin Chin.
Here is my laptop and the peace lily
I bought from Lloyd in the makeshift greenhouse,
the trains above making a muted racket.

Lloyd's black but he reminded me of you.
It was the way he managed the street shop
without seeming to manage it. His eyes,
kingpins, did not nail down my back and bag.

The plants around seemed to speak for him,
boxwood, snake plant, and bird of paradise,
as he transferred the lily to the black ceramic
pot and dish I had picked out. No charge,
Lloyd added, eyes smiling, for repotting it.

One leaf turned yellow yesterday. Dammit.

JEE LEONG KOH

Listening to Nouri al-Jarrah read from his book *A Boat to Lesbos*

"I wasn't in Damascus..."

I wasn't in Singapore when you weren't in Damascus.
I wasn't at home when you weren't at home.

I wasn't touching the patch of blood on the curtain
to see if it was wet, not when I wasn't in Damascus.

I couldn't explain my name to the American official
when you couldn't explain yours to the Greek.

My wife wasn't unravelling her shroud (I don't have a wife)
when your wife wasn't unravelling hers every night.

I wasn't Telemachus until you were Telemachus
when you weren't Telemachus until I was Telemachus.

My boat wasn't going anywhere fast as a bird
when your boat wasn't going anywhere fast as thought.

I wasn't Odysseus when you weren't Odysseus
but I was Odysseus when you were in Damascus.

SARAH GIRAGOSIAN

Salt Lick

You're my salt lick, and sometimes a white tail
hedging the dawn, and always a wild child,
standstill and spellbound in the forest,
translating blue-green moss and fern hair mood.
You're my snag at the heart, my cave of secrets,
and in the grotto the still, still pool. You're my season
of strawberries, my sun-bathing dreams.
You're that bolt of heat lightning, that flash within me.
You're a record of me, and I of you,
but in the years before the law let us marry,
we needed no proof. No stamp of approval.
And try as they did to part and reprove
us with DOMA, to tame our love with ICE,
we're the ecosystem that outlasts their cages;
we're the exchanges between wind, sea, and air.
But the fossils of your tears
crystalized inside me somewhere
after all those years of salt and waiting.

COURTNEY CONRAD

One More Gone Abroad

On Soup-Sundays: doors become steel pan drums,
potholes and cabs become roller coasters,
side streets become football pitches for sons,
elders play dominoes in crisp loafers.
Sweet joys do not overshadow terrors;
callous politicians create vultures,
possessions scatter on streets like feathers,
headlines battering youth for this culture.
Embassies bestowing visa blessings.
We flee, but resentment bottles tempers.
Years of souvenirs in barrels nestling,
the watering down of culture begins.
Flashing by, a rainbow of island stalls;
our mouths, sterilizing the word 'return'.

COURTNEY CONRAD

Motherland Nuh Want Wi Again
for Paulette Wilson

Rebuild
    rebuild
        rebuild

unnu hear weh di Queen of England seh?
she seh, come wid yuh madda, fadah, sista, bredda, and youngins.

Feet waddle and skip towards the ramp. Hands waving
goodbye to gulley pools, low hanging meals and soundclash
pickup trucks. Youngins crouch by their parent's feet, already
drawing postcards for their friends. Home: a cherry seed.

Bus drivers and cleaners kekek over once eating white rice
and honey; prepares to dab mouth corners and raise pinkies.
The ship docks, a new heat welcomes them.
Nurses' faces become sinks while emptying bedpans,
Cleaners sweep and mop charcoal and kerosine;
interfering with their own cremation. Riddling letters,
stuff envelopes inviting batons to dwarf self-worth.

Leave leave leave.

Unnu hear weh di Prime Minister seh?
She seh, guh back a yuh yard. Tek yuh madda,
fadah, sista, bredda, and youngins.

Flight BA 2263 to Jamaica is now boarding;
feet drag towards the gate. There is no slapdash
reunion, only stereos standing in the street
and a jerk cookout under the mango tree. Family
piles into chichi bus for a tour; pit stopping
to grin at old faces. Neighbours, *Pinkie, you dat?*
~~Yuh come back~~, *welcome home gyal.*

Restore restore restore.

JOSHUA ESCOBAR

A Developing Region

Accomplishments are advertised
Throughout the inland regions of southern California
Where industry buckled to dirt-jotted locales overflows
With a labor force from Guatemala Haiti Mexico Locus and Slover
American foreign affairs and the economy
Come together and collapse
Like cardboard boxes in the homes of
Newlyweds and refugees on the developing periphery
My best friend and I in his garage
Which had his teenage bed / couch and a TV
Define and defile
Whatever gives
Days definition
The way we crave
Contour and reaction
Language and the body
Dirtied by habit
Animals spend most of their time hiding
It's their #1 defence a volunteer said
At a park slated for development by a zoo
When no one's looking
People teenagers especially
Spend most of their time
Relishing a paradox
On the internet I can find only 1 or 2 photos of my teenage friend
Few exist online of socialites before digitization
Warehouses surrounded by stucco'd homes
The neighborhoods I grew up in sprawled onto the Jurupa hills
Unremarkable by most people's standards
Recently new warehouses were built over houses decades old
Technically part of no city
Their owners aren't actually people
An entity would develop warehouses for Amazon Sketchers Frito-Lay etc.
Throughout the poorer parts of a region called the Inland Empire.

SANJANA BIJLANI

Notes on translation

I write you in a language I have only voiced in brief, necessary exchanges: songs saved for Sundays, one-liners from movies, directions to the bathroom, the bus stop, nothing serious. If I get it wrong, the moment's already gone. The mistake doesn't leave a mark. I try to be accurate, but mostly I blush, fumble through. When I write you, I am promising a lifetime of never getting it right. More than half the premise of translation, love, is the certain risk of failure, a rowboat studded with holes. I begin slowly: *Hello*, not *Dear*. The rest, the middle, a growing puddle. I sign off *Good luck* so you can hear my laughter as I extend an oar, my hand. Let's exchange easy secrets. Let's float together. Let's stay here. There's something about the way you remind me of somewhere I can never return.

ALTON MELVAR M DAPANAS

Shubar Session at Rotonda

*Shubar (n.) refers to cigarette in the northern Mindanao Cebuano
Binisaya variant of Filipino gayspeak*

Such is the curse of this place: if you close your eyes, it disappears.
— Conchitina Cruz

Around us, this city of "golden friendship" revels on the mundane: the
rhythm of cicadas, occasional floods, and a drizzle, thin needles of shame,
baptizing us into believing the myth that we are still welcome here,
force-feeding guilt into our pores.

You take the air in, sucking it for life, then draw out smoke that was inside
you. The lighter's flame, brief as we were, hinted the scar of your lean
forearm, its skin-rivulet running through your beard, its point of origin. I
blew mine, a trail of smoke blending with the mist of December evening.
Your round brown eyes in the mottled light of passing vehicles, a museum
of contrast against the jaundiced glow of the concrete.

This is a curious case of exile: How can we want to leave when we are
already gone? But here we are again, in our usual haunts: our refuge
kilometer zero on seething holiday midnights—De Kalsada, CDO Bar,
Chill Corner, the fourth bridge from Macajalar Bay.

Up above, a skein of birds on top of a pavilion then to a lone tree. Down
below, here, we lean against your car trunk, our footwear on a cul-de-sac
wet with canal water. It seems that the light-years of our absence thin
into itself as we emerge as bodies that still ache towards leaving.

There is no return. We have become what this city wanted us to be:
gone.

ALTON MELVAR M DAPANAS

Scene: Portrait of Hungarian Boy
For Maaravi SH

This Pacific downpour, an outline, a yearning for heat.

How many graveyards for this boning?

And by landscape, I do not mean our native scenery: leis of jasmine, an
Amorsolo painting, seagulls against sunset, even coconut fronds.

It is this — how you pronounce sunset in Romani, hot springs in Budapest,
brands of pear liquor, years of Russian regime, wintry snow, the Jewish
origin of your name.
Teach me,
> I who know only know the tropics, its wet and dry seasons.

But how will I tell you about my forsaken demons as they dig their way up,
regaining their dominion?

I dare you, blonde boy with green irises, to only want, not remorse.

Plant my remains in a coffer, mark it three:
> — a reminder how we once had the alibi of touch
> — a testament that even this wreckage is something to look at
> — a covenant for us to never come back

JOHN MCCULLOUGH

Error Garden

Here, the vending machines are angels.
They flare beside shut salons and noodle bars in Shinjuku,
confronting the night, slicing paths through September's sticky heat.
I need all the help I can get. Striding down back streets,
I blunder round my head. A German word for *maze* captures it:
irrgarten, error garden.
                              Thinking is always chasing,
the mind approaches then loses impossible quarries—
a sequence of stumbling phrases, grasping air.

We left England because my hunts had grown dangerous,
a fretful slamming into walls, faster and harder, heart crashing,
snatching at breath.
                      In Shinjuku, other barriers surprise me
though already this is exoticized. Say it: walls of heat, walls of rain.

Clear umbrellas are popular. People stare up at what's falling
relentlessly toward them. Folk stories depict kasa-obake,
umbrella spirits with single eyes and long tongues
that bounce on one leg.
                          Words are the same. First, they offer shelter,
then they spring out at 4 am, won't stop opening, closing.

De Bono says most errors in thinking are *inadequacies
of perception*, not logic, but some failures of discernment

are beautiful. In Hama-rikyū Gardens, you strolled around with a soul
on your cap, a black butterfly with a row of fluorescent blue panels
on each wing, slipping into turquoise near the tips . . .

JOHN MCCULLOUGH

The latest wall of rain's ploughed off so I drape my jacket
over one arm, a tired spectre. It's not easy to stay vaporous
when each day, you present new windows on my life.
When I gaze through, shapes clarify, colours deepen.

Time to return to our hotel where you lie curled in your dressing gown.
Time to exchange words and atoms by the yellow blaze
of the vending machine that hovers outside our room,

your fingertips skimming slowly along my neck like a butterfly
that pauses to taste promising ground.

JOHN MCCULLOUGH

A Brief Chronicle of Panic

1900   Arthur Conan Doyle catches fire at Lord's when a cricket ball
        clouts the matchbox in his pocket

1909   A field mouse dodges between the spinning wheels of three
        carriages, vanishes under a door.

1918   Dr Yealland stubs out cigarettes on an ex-soldier's tongue, applies
        electric shocks to the back of his throat. *And still the coward clings to
        his disease of manhood.*

1932   On a crowded train platform, two maids in dancing heels on their
        night off clack along the edge.

1945   The bank clerk stays under his sheets, iron teeth champing, the
        rowdy sailor who shared his bed gone for good.

1965   A cockroach scrapes a policeman's boot, hurtles away to wash.

1987   At the rumour of thunder, the Pole who served with the German army
        pulls up the zip of his tent still positioned by the ring road.

1999   A literature professor looks herself up on the net, finds a woman in
        Texas with the same name poisoned a family with cyanide.

2002   Every plane the intern sees makes him feel all sizzle, skitter, tentacle.

2020   A jogger in Hove distractedly presses a crossing button, detonates
        into sweat.

2022   Shark skin under an electron microscope shows pointed scales: a
        street covered in flexing spikes. Behind the big teeth always, the little
        teeth.

LEAH COWAN

Baldwin Across Borders
'Where would a fleeing black man go?'

I'm watching a TV interview on a Dutch current affairs show with the writer James Baldwin from 1989, the same year the Berlin Wall fell, and a man carrying two shopping bags faced down tanks in Tiananmen Square. Air brittle with revolutions and deconstructions. In the interview, with his characteristic profound sensibility, words shattering air as warning shots expelled from the barrel of a pistol, Baldwin states that the entitlement to violence which white supremacy presumes for black people, is a myth. What's more, Baldwin explains, thoughts unfolding with careful precision as canvas unwrapped from a scalpel, our entitlement is to the lands and resources that were taken from us.

Part of the remarkable quality of Baldwin's writing is how he slides with darting, dancing fluidity between love and rage. His novels such as *Giovanni's Room* (1956), *Another Country* (1962) and *If Beale Street Could Talk* (1974) explore the almost arbitrary double-sided coin of care and cruelty; his essay collections such as *Notes of a Native Son* (1955) present a collage of anecdotes on this theme spanning American pop culture and police brutality in Paris, laced with the writer's inimitable sardonic sensibility. Baldwin's words do not so much straddle a duality between these modes of compassion and disconnection, but invite us to understand that the two are inextricably linked. A common position along this well-trodden route is one of pity. Addressing his white interviewer, he remarks:

> "All you really have, after all, are space shuttles, banks and weapons. What you don't have any more, is me. I, the slave. I, the n*gger. I, the black cat who believed everything you said...once."

His ability to understand this complexity is rooted in his experience as a queer black man trying to survive in America. For Baldwin, it is very much a question of mere survival. As prison abolitionist and scholar Ruth Wilson Gilmore explains, racism, at the end of it all, is the "state-sanctioned or extralegal production and exploitation of group-differentiated vulnerability to premature death". The political theory which underpins Baldwin's work is unflinching in recognising how centuries of inequality carry a deep legacy into the present day.

LEAH COWAN

Back to the TV interview, Baldwin's words are a talisman against cold mists:

"You wrecked our neighbourhoods before we were compelled to come here and wreck your neighbourhoods...you discovered us, and now you got us."

This aphorism produces a drumbeat I recognise. I picture, instantly, the words leaping from his mouth and congealing into a shining string, springing out of Haarlem in the Netherlands and soaring through time and space to connect directly with a multitude of voices, accelerating a pulsing thrum of decolonial thought. Baldwin's words touch down on rainy asphalt somewhere near King's Cross station, slip through the back door of the Institute of Race Relations and join hands with then Director A. Sivanandan's aphorism "We are here because you were there". This sojourn retraces journeys made by Baldwin a few decades before: in 1965 and 1968 he visits London, by chance the two years in which Martin Luther King, Jr. and Malcolm X were murdered. Two shimmering points in the history of black struggle.

From London, this foundational missive takes the red-eye to Santa Cruz, landing on the front doorstep of Chicana lesbian poet and fiction writer Gloria Anzaldúa, where among weeds and wilted blueberry bushes it meets with the unequivocal incantation: "This land was Mexican once, was Indian always and is. And will be again." Like Anzaldúa, who excavates the ubiquitous, all-encompassing nature of the "psychological borderlands, the sexual borderlands and the spiritual borderlands", Baldwin examines the divisions that fester within hearts and minds as a result of long histories of geopolitical line-carving. Baldwin does not write about borders of barbed wire, boats and document checks. He writes of fences within and between us on a visceral level; of humanity's disconnection from itself. In an 1962 essay for the New Yorker, he laments that:

"It will be a great day for America, incidentally, when we begin to eat bread again, instead of the blasphemous and tasteless foam rubber that we have substituted for it [...] Something very sinister happens to the people of a country when they begin to distrust their own reactions as deeply as they do here, and become as joyless as they have become. It is this individual uncertainty [...] that makes the discussion, let alone elucidation, of any conundrum—that is, any reality—so supremely difficult."

For Baldwin, the inedibility of daily bread in America, this quotidian process of connecting inside stomach to outside world, is disturbingly insipid. His distaste for bad bread reveals not only the legacy of his years frequenting the boulangeries of Paris, but also the revelation that disconnection from the self prevents social progress. Baldwin reveals to us a great chasm between humans, one blockaded with fabrications and untruths which prop up structures of inequality. His writings become an interlocutor. His words are borrowed credentials for crossing perilous borderlands.

In 1948, Baldwin left America and took up writing in France. In France, he felt he had more breathing space and creative capacity to think and write, removed from the "real social danger visible in the face of every cop, every boss, everybody" which he experienced in the US. In *James Baldwin in Paris*, a documentary short made in 1970, Baldwin explains his exodus, remarking that "I knew I was gonna be murdered there [...] I mean that I could not have hoped to live if I had stayed there". This subtle clarification is crucial - physical death is not necessarily what Baldwin seeks to avoid, or believes he can ever circumnavigate, but he flees the living death of constant surveillance and scrutiny, wishes to dispense with the energy exerted through continually bracing for violence, and not being able to turn his full attention to writing. Baldwin practices the act of border-crossing to find a freedom of sorts. As he reminds the crowd in a speech at London's West Indian Centre in 1968: "[freedom] may not be as real as slavery, which is a very concrete thing, but freedom is what one's after". Yet he is clear that freedom is found in the crossing and not the arrival. In the documentary short, rebutting the suggestion that he has 'escaped' racism by leaving America, he poses the question: "Where would a fleeing black man go if he wanted to escape?".

Throughout all, Baldwin nonetheless reinforces the generative power of struggle across boundaries within and outside of us, in paradox with his consistent disdain for the fabrication of self-delusion with which whiteness bloats itself. He shares with faith and fire his absolute commitment to justice for black people. As Anzaldúa writes, "There are compensations for this mestiza, and certain joys. Living on borders and in margins, keeping intact one's shifting and multiple identity and integrity, is like trying to swim in a new element, an "alien" element". Baldwin embodies this, and scribes the knowledge produced in the borderlands. He is never idealistic, but coolly optimistic, a warrior surveying a small arsenal and knowing there can be no other way. "The world is held together by the love and the passion of a very few people" he remarks in the documentary short. Baldwin's words are the hushed crackle of a needle landing on a record, weighted with mourning for our premature deaths, then propelled through the cyclical rhythm of lives lived in spite of it all.

JAY G YING

Talos

If I could kill you I would then have to make another exactly like you.
—Anne Carson

I printed my head from the mirror-map of this island with no name.

I travelled into the translated nation where moonlight fell on my skin like unconsenting magnesium. I always itched to be inside out, longed for new metals to attach onto these hands of flaring fires, golden hair, platinum body, bronze wings, tears of mercury.

A coppery skin laid out on the hostel bed for me to try on.

My old mortal hips were useless souvenirs I wanted to smuggle onto the island. I could not resist the vibrations of the scanning instruments when I let myself be captured.

In my cell, I dreamt I really did empty all that connective and unused tissue behind; what a joy to just linger in the dampness of my hot and dirty organs, growing as mould does for one mythical second.

I was an automaton box, as lifelike as an empire opening up its ruins.

So when I lowered my shelled out spaces onto your doctor's tray I did not do it alphabetically, nor by their distances to the steel autopsy table, not by their utilities, their histories of malfunction.

I balanced their wet waking against my third spaces, adopting a scale only known to the dead.

I arranged my organs like a child, so naturally, without even needing to use the brain you first removed; the old method came to me, reminding me of imported dolls I used to play with. I was waiting for my input, aching for orientation.

I was asking to be represented.

JAY G YING

And your knife's sweaty condensation, I must admit, was barely chilled at all when you teased it across my navel, ready to carve your initials, or some other ideogram emptied of all its ancient meanings.

You thought I could not see the humanitarian in the shimmering reflection of your blade, eyeing my insides up. The lusting worm inside my plastic skull asked if I really belonged in this story.

All along you lacked the critical imagination to know that I was always conscious of your presence, my absence, as I waited for that quick metal twist.

Your machines burrowed deeper into my bronze flesh, your grief exploding as
a million scars over my skin until it became a soft and blank surface again.

You could write a book with all those secrets of alchemy you reverse engineered.

You worked hard to make it work, and I was glad it did, even though so much blood was drained.

My pumped molten ichor rushed to stain the sand outside with its novelty, like a rainstorm that cannot cease its own exhaustion.

Everything the lead animates on the island becomes coated in a winking reflection. Every person the reflection touches becomes a ghost glowing in the distance, circling the island's shore, unsure of the life they now haunt, unsure about what they are meant to protect.

I want to speak out but find I have no voice box, only a reel of memories I shuffle from the right order into the wrong.

XIMENA KEOGH SERRANO

Formations
Para Mamá

You remember that return like the beginning. You remember the delicate traces of your mother's stance then, when she barely weighed 90 pounds and your rosy cheeks couldn't get enough bread. The starch of ignorance feeding your face. The flesh-sucking ills of two fatherless homes hanging over mamá's skin. You were ten years old then. Already a child strung between nations, already a champion in the art of resilience and flight. You, so very well trained in the ways of the chameleon.

*

Your name in full is a speech act in movement. It requires a certain malleability of the tongue. It requires a hunger for moons and curious arms always ready to swing, open.

*

There are life moments that sit over your retina like a translucent veil, marking your step, always there, always hanging around, seeking for you to notice. But the traps of forced ceguera have long clung to your membranes. Its halls so deep, that blinding glow!

J.P. DER BOGHOSSIAN

Those Words You Can't Find in a Dictionary

I absconded from my grandmother's living room with my grandfather Michel's French-Armenian dictionary, a hardback volume with a rusty red linen cover. I had filched it off the side table, carried it behind me to the guest bedroom, opened my frayed black nylon suitcase, and slid the dictionary underneath my boxer briefs. A peculiar intimacy—my grandfather's words wrapped in my underwear.

I have no memories of Michel. He died when I was eleven, and I was on the other side of the Atlantic, and hadn't seen him since I was eight. I have photos of various trips to France to visit him and the family. One small square photo is from a trip in June 1984 to celebrate my third birthday. He sits in a lawn chair - square jaw and a well fed stomach - wearing wide glasses from the 1970s and a tan fedora. I splash around in a two-foot wide enamel wash tub, filled with about six inches of water. I hold up an empty plastic cup, with a curious smile, soaked hair, and browning skin.

Mysteries barricade Michel from me. The language barrier for one. We both came to French as our second language. In 1984, I would have spoken English with a sprinkle of French vocabulary, and he would have spoken Armenian with proficient French. Myriam claimed Michel was born in Armenia, but my grandmother said Artsakh. He served in the Soviet Army during World War II, but how he made it to France is unclear, or unspoken of. Something to do with the Nazis. After the war Michel had made his way to Valence, met my grandmother, married, and had five children. He worked at a dry cleaners. Years later, he revealed to the children that he had a previous wife and daughter, who still lived in Armenia. I do not know if his wife and child attempted to join him in France, and if so, how the Soviet government prevented this, or who convinced whom that Michel should remarry, but they couldn't get out, and he did remarry, and he sent them money for decades. He died the year Armenia declared its independence.

A man named Armande bought the dictionary in Paris. I'm uncertain of Armande's relationship to Michel. The family tree is knotty in the thicket of in-laws. Armande inscribed the book, "To Michel Der Boghossian, as a sign of friendship and affection in order to maintain our roots."

There was no table of contents, so Michel wrote one in red ink and protected it with clear tape. On the inside cover, he wrote his telephone number in pencil and red ink. He signed the title page as *M D Boghossian*. He underlined dozens of words. Most of them don't seem to suggest anything beyond a man learning a second language: *assidu* (constant), *débarquer* (disembark). He starred the word *granit* (granite). I wonder what urgency had required him to star granite, the only word to receive such importance. Some underlined words did suggest something of his interests: *repeçêher* and *hamecon*, to fish and fishhook. He underlined *glycémie* (blood sugar). Diabetes is a prominent risk factor for having a stroke. While hospitalized for one, he caught the infection that took his life.

As his queer grandson, I inspected the dictionary to see if he had underlined gay or homosexual. But the publisher didn't include any of those words, nor did they include *bisexual* or *transgenre*. However, he had underlined *perversité* and *fornicateur*. I tried to imagine that maybe he had been bisexual or gay and that it was his shame who underlined those words. But that thought unnerved me. Would he have tried to stamp out in me what he knew in himself? A crushing thought when you're looking for a grandpa. I can't speak to why Michel even needed the dictionary. By 1984, he must have spoken fluent French. Perhaps Armande's "sign of friendship and affection" was to gently engage a Michel who still struggled with the language. But, Armande also wrote, "in order to maintain our roots." Perhaps Michel had started to forget his Armenian.

I keep my photo of him in the dictionary. The aesthetic of the picture is coherent, easily describable. A grandfather watching his grandson, golden splashes of sun, a lawn chair, playful smiles, a fedora hat. An aesthetic without the ambiguity of living in France as an Armenian man with Franco-Armenian children, and Armenian-American grandchildren, who so obviously looked Der Boghossian, but who visited with him in yet another language to surmount. I imagine him after the photo, returning inside, paging through his dictionary, finding himself surrounded by words, and yet mired in an indescribability—those words you can't find in a dictionary.

SHAYNA GEE

Pearl River Delta

everywhere in canton / the rivers break / at its throat / my ma says / i was born / head folded to my feet / yes / my ass came out first / plopped into the delta / boat woman / ham sui moi / watered me / gentled this skin with / salt water / nurtured / a pearl / so iridescent / they prayed / i / will still live by water / cure abandoned boats / wield blood to safe passages / *i'm only a pearl* / not yet a river / rivers everywhere / want your neck / sinking / tell me / does an egg still float without its shell / my ma / is a lousy swimmer / but her eyes / glided by moonbeam / can see / a blacken playground / and swear on boats / the pearl she saw / waiting like appetite

TAYLOR JOHNSON

States of decline

The room is dying honey and lemon rind.
Soured light. My grandmother sits in her chair

sweetening into the blue velvet. Domestic
declension is the window that never opens—

the paint peeling, dusting the sill, and inhaled.
It is an american love she lives in,

my grandmother, rigored to televangelists
and infomercials. Losing the use of her legs.

Needing to be turned like a mattress.
No one is coming for her. The dog is

asleep in the yard, Her husband,
obedient to the grease and garlic.

TAYLOR JOHNSON

Virginia Slim

Young buck tapping
its velvet against the
bathroom window in
the morning. The land
leaning in the pines,
the well, cattails,
muscadines, hot metal
in the shed, chicory on
the stove at twilight. In
the orange morning
I rose w/ my grandfather,
with the larger animals
of our imagination, and
warmed the truck to go
to the water. On the way
I laid down in the truck
bed and caught a rabbit
barely in the grasp of a
hawk. What did I know
about being hunted? I
knew everything. The
meek don't inherit
shit— I stuffed
my mouth with pine needles
and spit, bled and spit,
at the root, and look
where it's got me—
landless. If the water
was a myth, then I went
in looking for my dog
only to find my
grandmother's armchair.
I rode it as I would any
wet story— to deeper
blue. Listen: by

TAYLOR JOHNSON

Virginia Slim

lamplight my
grandfather would lead
me to the edge of the
woods— *this is yours*—
then he would kill the
light. If I told you he
flew back to his house,
what are you supposed
to believe; it was just
me and my green hope
pressing through the
black. How else am I
supposed to enter the
world if I'd already left
once: as myth: not set
apart: but as a small
shelled thing: low:
toiling in the dirt: lifting
every bit of black to
breathe

TAYLOR JOHNSON

On my way to you

Everyday is an invitation into intimacy, I decide, leaving my house.
That I would cross it, given the distance. Being money myself
and having none in the form of new shoes and all these holes in my jacket.
I inherited this privacy, given what it's like to be an instrument—

Given each plant singing in its season. Given the trees between.
How can I tell you, given that you abide, I zeroed out in the field.
Given the no place of the soul. Given the soul ringing in the forest's
hollows. Given to ringing, being money myself given away.

Given the language this image system produces. Given that distance.
Given how maroon the morning war sky I wake up in,
owning nothing being money myself. Given that the block is mine
sayeth the red-eyed gods slouched over standing up in exquisite coats.

Given trouble and home in the city that slipped out one night.
Given Uptown, Trinidad, KDY, wolves in Rock Creek. Given to corn-syrup
spilling out the cornerstore. Given the technicolor hole of the cornerstore.
Given 7th &Florida, that chromophonic praise break at the intersection.
Given that happenstance touch.

Given the distance of money, I'm from nowhere where I'm from.
Being not monied myself and given to language. Given and being let go.
That distance. That I could cross it, given that you can hear me.

Afterword

KAZIM ALI

How can one even live as queer? To me "queer" means to live against the guidance, rules, and claims of any structure that came before. A rejection of not necessarily the metaphors and concepts (church, law, and coin) but a meaningful and sustained confrontation with the motivating values: that one must live by another's moral rules, that one's physical body can be controlled by violence (behind every government and every law is the inherent threat of violence for non-compliance), and a subscription to all the exquisite fictions and lies required by the tenuous and unsustainable structures of global capitalism and empire.

Queerness moves boldly past the routines and repetitions, and into *experience* itself. Maybe queers leave home or queer home because we have to find what is beyond the ordinary, beyond the normative. We do not have homes. We must make and build our own or embrace the road and roof of stars. We cross borders without papers. We are already in between, always beyond. How then to live? None of the traditions that exist can help us. Queerness requires we cannot answer but similarly requires that we do beg the question.

These are the poets who invent themselves in language, in bodily experience, in breath moving into expression. Here then are the words that could help you live. Read them out loud, draw them on another's body in ink or saliva or sweat. Make them live and love. And then, best of all, write your own lyrics, sing with the music of the one life you have, make of the space of your days a choreography no one could match.

About the contributors

Kazim Ali is a poet, writer, academic and activist. He is the author of numerous poetry collections, essays, and works in translations. His newest books are a volume of three long poems *The Voice of Sheila Chandra* (Platypus Press, 2021) and a memoir of his Canadian childhood, *Northern Light* (Milkweed Press, 2021). In 2003 Ali co-founded Nightboat Books. Ali lives in California and is chair of the Department of Literature at the University of California, San Diego.

Sanjana Bijlani writes with questions of care, memory, and belonging in the Indian diaspora. Her writing appears in *Wildness, Cream City Review, Scum,* and elsewhere.

Jody Chan is a writer, drummer, organiser, and therapist based in Toronto. They are the author of *sick* (Black Lawrence, 2020), winner of the 2018 St. Lawrence Book Award, *all our futures* (PANK, 2020) and *haunt* (Damaged Goods, 2018).

Mary Jean Chan is the author of *Flèche* (Faber & Faber, 2019), winner of the 2019 Costa Poetry Award and shortlisted for the 2020 International Dylan Thomas Prize and the Seamus Heaney Centre First Collection Poetry Prize. Chan is Senior Lecturer in Creative Writing (Poetry) at Oxford Brookes University and tutors on the MSt in Creative Writing at the University of Oxford. She is a contributing editor at Oxford Poetry.

Courtney Conrad is a Jamaican poet. She is a member of Malika's Poetry Kitchen and an alumna of the Obsidian Foundation Retreat and Roundhouse Poetry Collective. She has performed at various festivals and her work has been published by Bad Betty Press, *Birmingham Literary Journal* and *The White Review.* She was shortlisted for The White Review Poet's Prize 2020 and longlisted for the Rebecca Swift Women Poets' Prize 2020.

About the contributors

Leah Cowan is a writer and editor living in London. She is the author of *Border Nation: A Story of Migration* (Pluto Press 2021). She speaks on race, gender and migration. Her writing has been published by the *Guardian, Red Pepper, Dazed* and *DOPE Magazine.*

Alton Melvar M Dapanas is the author of *Towards a Theory on City Boys* (Newcomer Press, 2021), assistant creative nonfiction editor of *Panorama: The Journal of Intelligent Travel* and *Atlas & Alice Literary Magazine.* Their work has appeared in international publications. They're from Metro Cagayan de Oro in southern Philippines.

J.P. Der Boghossian is the founder of the Queer Armenian Library. He is the President of the Armenian Cultural Organization of Minnesota and a board member of the International Armenian Literary Alliance. His essay will be published in a forthcoming anthology of Armenian American writers.

Joshua Escobar is the author of *Bareback Nightfall* (Noemi Press, 2020) and performs as DJ Ashtrae + Little Piñata. He grew up in southern California's Inland Empire. He teaches at Santa Barbara City College.

Shayna Gee is a writer living in the Bay Area. They're the author of *Mushrooms At The E-Grave* (Ghost City, 2021). Their work has appeared or is forthcoming in Bell Press, Stone of Madness Press, *West Trestle Review, Write Now! SF Bay,* and elsewhere. They read for *Homology Lit* and *the winnow.*

Sarah Giragosian is a poet and critic living in Schenectady, NY. She is the author of the poetry collections *Queer Fish* (Dream Horse, 2017), winner of the American Poetry Journal Book Prize, *The Death Spiral* (Black Lawrence, 2020) and co-editor (with Virginia Konchan) of *Marbles on the Floor: How to Assemble a Book of Poems* (University of Akron Press, forthcoming). Her writing has appeared in *Orion, Ecotone, Tin House,* and *Prairie Schooner,* among others.

About the contributors

Noor Hindi is a Palestinian-American poet and reporter. Her poems have appeared or are forthcoming in *Poetry, Hobart* and *Jubilat*. Her essays have appeared or are forthcoming in *American Poetry Review, Literary Hub,* and *Adroit Journal.* Hindi is the Equity and Inclusion Reporter for *The Devil Strip Magazine.*

Taylor Johnson is the author of *Inheritance* (Alice James Books, 2020). Their work appears in *The Paris Review, The Baffler, Scalawag,* and elsewhere. Johnson is a Cave Canem Fellow and a recipient of the 2017 Larry Neal Writers' Award from the DC Commission on the Arts and Humanities. They live in New Orleans where they listen.

Diana Khoi Nguyen is a poet and multimedia artist. She is the author of *Unless* (Belladonna*, 2019) and *Ghost Of* (Omnidawn 2018), which was selected by Terrance Hayes for the Omnidawn Open Contest, and was a finalist for the National Book Award and received the 2019 Kate Tufts Discovery Award and Colorado Book Award. Her poetry and prose have appeared in *Poetry, American Poetry Review, PEN America,* and elsewhere. A Kundiman fellow, she teaches at Randolph College and is an Assistant Professor at the University of Pittsburgh.

Golnoosh Nour is a writer, editor and educator living in London. She is the author of *The Ministry of Guidance and Other Stories.* Her poetry collection *Rocksong* will be published in October 2021 by Verve Poetry Press. She is the co-editor of *Magma 80* and the anthology *Queer Life, Queer Love* forthcoming with Muswell Press. Her writing and poetry translations have appeared in *Granta, Columbia Journal, Poetry Anthology,* and elsewhere. She teaches Creative Writing at the University of Reading.

Jee Leong Koh is a poet and essayist. He is the author of *Conor & Seal - A Harlem Story in 47 Poems* (Sibling Rivalry, 2020) and *Steep Tea* (Carcanet, 2015), a Finalist by Lambda Literary Awards. He has published four other books of poems and a book of zuihitsu. Originally from Singapore, Koh lives in New York City, where he runs Singapore Unbound and the indie press Gaudy Boy.

About the contributors

Andriniki Mattis is a non-binary poet, who has received fellowships from Cave Canem, Poets House and The Poetry Project. They earned an MA in Creative Writing and Education, from Goldsmiths University of London, and a BA in Political and Poetic Resistance, from Brooklyn College.
Their work has appeared in *Nepantla, Cortland Review, Typo Mag, THEM journal*, and elsewhere. Andriniki is from and lives in Brooklyn.

John McCullough is the author of *Reckless Paper Birds* (Penned in the Margins, 2019), winner of the 2020 Hawthornden Prize for Literature, for overall best UK book of the year and shortlisted for the Costa Poetry Award. His first collection *The Frost Fairs* (Salt, 2011) won the Polari First Book Prize. He teaches creative writing at the University of Brighton, the Arvon Foundation and New Writing South, and lives in Hove, England.

Xandria Phillips is a poet and visual artist from rural Ohio. Xandria is the author of *HULL* (Nightboat Books, 2019), winner of the 2020 Judith A. Markowitz Award for Emerging Writers and a Lambda Literary Award. They have received numerous fellowships and a 2021 Whiting Award in Poetry. Their poetry has been published in *American Poetry Review, BOMB, Black Warrior Review, Crazyhorse,* and elsewhere.

Peter Scalepllo is a queer poet and sexual health therapist from Glasgow. He is the author of *Acting Out and chem & other poems* (Broken Sleep Books, 2021), his writing has been published internationally.

Jay G Ying is a Chinese-Scottish writer and MFA student at Brown University. He is the author of *Wedding Beasts* (Bitter Melon, 2019), short listed for the Saltire-Calum MacDonald Award, and *Katabasis* (The Poetry Business, 2020), winner of a New Poets Prize. He is a Contributing Editor at *The White Review*, and reviews for *Harriet Books* at the Poetry Foundation. His work appears in *Granta, Modern Poetry in Translation, The Poetry Review* and elsewhere.

Acknowledgements

I am grateful for all the people who have supported the very dream, idea and realisation of Anamot Press. In particular, Eve Avdoulos for her creativity and encouragement. Matthias Kispert for editing the first video recording to launch the Poetry Streaming Series. Leah Cowan for listening, reading and reminding me how to be shamelessly true to my values and vision for Anamot Press. Before producing this anthology, I was particularly inspired by a workshop led by Bad Betty Press during Free Verse Poetry Fair 2020, working with the Poetry Translation Centre and reading *An Anthology for Queer Poets of Colour* edited by Christopher Soto (Nightboat Books, 2018). The production and first print-run of this book has been made possible through a generous grant from Arts Council England.

I'm in awe of and grateful for the twenty writers who have trusted their work to be part of this anthology. Thanks also goes to all the contributors to the Anamot Press Poetry Streaming Series, especially Raymond Antrobus and Mary Jean Chan for being the first two writers to share a recorded reading in the first week of the UK national lockdown.

Thank you for your generosity and guidance Robin Silas Christian, James Trevelyan, Michael Schmidt, Niall Munro, Holly Ovenden. In particular, Yannick Scott who has provided in-kind design support form the beginning and illustrated the cover of this book.

Thank you to my family and friends for their love. Lastly, a special thank you to my mum for introducing me to poetry and reading Paruyr Sevak to me.

Credits

"Ode to Self" by Golnoosh Nour, previously published online in July 2020, *Issue 2 of The Signal House Edition* (www.signalhouseedition.org/issue2poetry), is reproduced by permission of the author.

"semantic satiation" and "palinode" by Jody Chan, published in *sick* (Black Lawrence Press, 2020), are reproduced by permission of the author.

"Want Could Kill Me", "Poem Where I Refuse To Talk About" and "You and I" by Xandria Phillips, published in *HULL* (Nightboat Books, 2019), are reproduced by permission of the author.

"Gyotaku" and "I Keep Getting Things Wrong" by Diana Khoi Nguyen, published in *Ghost Of* (Omnidawn Publishing, 2018), are reproduced by permission of the author and publisher.

"States of decline", "Virginia Slim" and "On my way to you" by Taylor Johnson, published in *Inheritance* (Alice James Books, 2020), are reproduced by permission of the author.

"Scene: Portrait of Hungarian Boy" by Alton Melvar M Dapanas, previously published online in March 2021, *Issue 2: t4t of Delicate Friend* (www.delicatefriend.com/alton-melvar-m-dapanas), is reproduced by permission of the author.